Amazing Americans

Rosa Parks

Kristin Kemp, M.A.E.

Consultant

Caryn Williams, M.S.Ed.
Madison County Schools
Huntsville, AL

Image Credits: Cover, pp.1, 4 William Philpott/Reuters/Newscom; p.12 Everett Collection Inc/Alamy; p.18 Gene Herrick/Associated Press; p.23 (top) Jim McKnight/Associated Press; p.7 The Bridgeman Art; p.25 (top) David Tulis/Bettmann/Corbis; pp.9, 19 Bettmann/Corbis; p.27 (top) Chuck Kennedy/MCT/Getty Images; p.22 Don Cravens/Time & Life Pictures/Getty Images; p.21 Ed Clark/Time & Life Pictures/Getty Image; p.8 FPG/Archive Photos/Getty Images; p.24 (left) Francis Miller/Time & Life Pictures/Getty Images; p.24 (right) Paul Schutzer/Time & Life Pictures/Getty Image; p.14 Stan Wayman/Time & Life Pictures/Getty Image; p.15 (background) Tony Vaccaro/Archive Photos/Getty Images; p.28 (top) Dr. Judy Hung; pp.10–11(all) Jack Delano/The Granger Collection, NYC/Granger Collection; p.12 LOC, LC-DIG-fsa-8a26761, pp.2–3 LOC, LC-USZ62-126840, p.20 LOC, LC-USZ62-111235, p.13 LOC, LC-USZ62-116817, pp.5, 32 LOC, LC-DIG-ppmsca-03128, p.15 (top) LOC, na0108p1 The Library of Congress; pp.6 (left), 31 akg-images/Newscom; p.16 Everett Collection/Newscom; p.26 TRIPPETT/SIPA/Newscom; p.25 World History Archive/Newscom; p.17 (left) ZUMA Press/Newscom; pp.28–29 Scott Vaughan; pp.3, 17 (botom) Wikimedia Common; all other images from Shutterstock.

Library of Congress Cataloging-in-Publication Data

Kemp, Kristin.
    Amazing Americans: Rosa Parks / Kristin Kemp, M.A.E.
        pages cm
    Includes index.
    Audience: Grades K-3.
    ISBN 978-1-4333-7375-6 (pbk.)
    ISBN 978-1-4807-5161-3 (ebook)
    1. Parks, Rosa, 1913-2005—Juvenile literature.
    2. African American women—Alabama—Montgomery—Biography—Juvenile literature. 3. African Americans—Alabama—Montgomery—Biography—Juvenile literature.
    4. Civil rights workers—Alabama—Montgomery—Biography—Juvenile literature. 5. African Americans—Civil rights—Alabama—Montgomery—History—20th century—Juvenile literature. 6. Segregation in transportation—Alabama—Montgomery—History—20th century—Juvenile literature. 7. Montgomery (Ala.)—Race relations—Juvenile literature. 8. Montgomery (Ala.)—Biography—Juvenile literature.
    I. Title. II. Title: Rosa Parks.
    F334.M753P38477 2015
    323.092—dc23
    [B]
                                2014010606

Teacher Created Materials

5301 Oceanus Drive
Huntington Beach, CA 92649-1030
http://www.tcmpub.com

ISBN 978-1-4333-7375-6

Table of Contents

Sparking a Movement

Many people know the name Rosa Parks. She reminds people of an unfair time for African Americans. There were many laws that made African Americans feel that they were not **equal** to whites. The laws said that they needed to use separate restrooms and drinking fountains. They could not go to the same schools. They could not sit in the same movie theaters or eat in the same restaurants. African Americans wanted the laws to change. They wanted to be treated fairly.

Parks wanted the laws to change, too. She was willing to stand up for herself to make it happen. Parks refused to give up her seat on a bus to a white man. That simple act began a great change in America. It sparked the **civil rights** movement.

Rosa Parks

People protest in the March on Washington for Jobs and Freedom in 1963.

Civil Rights Movement

The civil rights movement was the fight to give civil rights to African Americans. These are rights that all people should have, such as the right to be free, happy, and safe.

Young Parks

Rosa Parks was born on February 4, 1913. Her name was Rosa McCauley (muh-KAW-lee) before she was married. Her father was a carpenter. This is someone who builds things, such as homes and furniture. Her mother was a teacher. When Parks was two years old, her mother moved away with her and her younger brother. They lived with her grandparents in Pine Level, Alabama. They were poor, but Parks had fun on the farm. She played outside and did chores.

Alabama

Rosa Parks

Parks loved her family. She took care of her brother. Her mother took Parks to church and taught her to read. Her grandparents had been **slaves** when they were young. They told her stories about when they were kids. They taught her to be strong and to stand up for herself. She never forgot the things they told her.

Slaves

Slaves were people who had no freedom and were owned by other people. In 1865, the United States said people could not own slaves anymore.

In 1919, Parks started school. She loved learning, but she also noticed that things were unfair. Her school was only for African American students. It was one room that had one teacher and 50 students. Parks had to walk to school because there was no bus. And, her school was only open five months a year. The school for white students was very different. There were many teachers and classrooms. White students rode buses. And their school was open nine months a year.

The law said that African Americans and white people should be kept apart. This was called **segregation** (seg-ri-GEY-shuhn). The law also said that everything had to be equal. This idea was known as "separate but equal." But things were not equal.

White students often had better materials and smaller classes.

Parks went to a segregated school like this one.

In 1924, Parks finished sixth grade. She went to live with her aunt in Montgomery (mont-GUHM-uh-ree), Alabama. It had better schools for African American girls. Her new teachers were nice to her and believed in her. She learned math, science, and reading. She also learned to set goals for herself. Parks wanted to finish high school. At that time, not many African American girls did this.

segregated school

In 1929, Parks's grandmother became ill. Parks had to quit school to take care of her. But her grandmother passed away. Then, her mother became ill. Parks needed to make money to support her family, so she found a job cleaning houses. Parks was disappointed that she would not finish high school, but she wanted to do the right thing.

Parks worked cleaning houses like this one.

Getting Involved

When Parks was 18, she met a man named Raymond Parks. He asked her to marry him on their second date! Two years later, they got married. Raymond loved to read. He knew Parks was smart, too. He wanted her to go back to school. In 1932, she finished high school at the age of 19.

Raymond was a member of the National Association (uh-soh-see-EY-shuhn) for the Advancement (ad-VANS-muhnt) of Colored People (NAACP). At that time, people called African Americans "colored people." This group wanted to make things fair for African Americans.

This man drinks from a segregated water fountain.

Raymond was fighting for civil rights, and Parks wanted to get involved, too. She went to a meeting and she took notes about what the people said. She did a good job. The leader, E. D. Nixon, asked her to be the secretary. She would take notes at all of their meetings.

How Do You Say It?

The correct way to say NAACP is N-Double A-C-P. This group continues to fight for equality today.

These NAACP members protest segregation.

Parks liked working for the NAACP. It was hard work, but she felt like she was making a difference. African Americans were still not being treated equally. She wanted to help change that.

Parks was sad to see people segregated on buses. Only white people could sit in the front of the bus. The back of the bus was for African Americans, and the middle was for both. If African Americans were sitting in the middle and a white person wanted a seat, they had to move. Even getting on the bus was unfair. African Americans had to come in the front door of the bus to pay and then get off the bus and go to the back door to take a seat. They were not allowed to walk past white people. Parks knew that things had to change.

segregated bus

509

NO SMOKING

COLORED SEAT FROM REAR

This sign was posted in the front of buses during this time period.

Parks is fingerprinted at the police station after her arrest.

Respectful Rebel

On December 1, 1955, Parks got on the bus after work. She sat in the middle section where white people and African Americans could sit. As she rode, more and more people got on the bus. It was very crowded, and soon there were no seats left. A white man got on the bus and had to stand.

The law said that Parks had to give her seat to him, but she refused. The bus driver stopped the bus and told her to stand up. Parks was calm and polite, but she still refused to move. The bus driver called the police. A police officer came and told her to move or he would place her under arrest. She politely said, "You may do that." The police officer then arrested Parks.

Parks's picture is taken at the police station.

police report on Parks's arrest

Raymond came to pick up Parks at the police station. E. D. Nixon from the NAACP paid the **bail**. This was money that had to be paid before Parks could leave. She still had to go to **court**. A judge would decide if she had broken the law.

In court, the judge told Parks that she had to pay $14 for breaking the law. Parks refused to pay. Her case then went to higher courts. She was not about to give up now!

American Justice

Courts are where cases are heard. Judges listen to the cases and decide if someone broke the law. If someone thinks that a judge made a bad decision, he or she can have a judge in a higher court hear his or her case.

E. D. Nixon and Parks in court for Parks's trial.

Nixon and Parks knew that this could be the start of important changes. They wanted everyone in Montgomery to get involved. They decided to **boycott** the buses. They asked civil rights leader Dr. Martin Luther King Jr. to help. African Americans did not ride the buses until the law changed. This would make the bus companies lose money. So African Americans started walking instead of riding on the buses.

Parks also boycotted the busses. Here she is on her way to jail for the boycott.

Parks's case went all the way to the Supreme Court. This is the highest court in the United States. It decided that the law in Montgomery was unfair. Parks won her case! African Americans could now sit anywhere on a bus. On December 20, 1956, the boycott was finally over. African Americans had not ridden the bus in over a year!

Parks got on a bus for the first time after her arrest and sat in the front seat. A white man was sitting behind her. But now no one could tell her to sit in the back. She did not have to give up her seat. There were still many unfair laws for African Americans, but Parks knew that this was a good start. She wanted to keep fighting for civil rights.

Parks rides in the front of a bus after winning her case.

Famous Lawyer

The **lawyer** that helped Parks win her case was Thurgood Marshall. He was a famous civil rights leader. He fought against unfair laws for African Americans. He was a lawyer, a judge, and even the first African American Supreme Court justice.

Parks works as a seamstress.

A New Start

After the boycott, things were difficult for Raymond and Parks. Some people did not want African Americans to have civil rights. Raymond and Parks could not find jobs. Angry people sent them mean letters and Parks received rude phone calls.

Raymond decided that they needed to move away. They moved to Detroit, Michigan, where Parks's brother lived. He helped them find a new home. Parks found a sewing job and got involved in a local church.

Parks at work for John Conyers Jr. in 1971.

In 1964, an African American man from Detroit was **elected** to **Congress**. This is the group that makes our country's laws. His name was John Conyers (KAHN-yuhrz) Jr. Parks went to work for him. She liked her job a lot. She worked for him for many years.

23

Laws were changing all over the country. Parks gave speeches. She shared her story with people. In 1963, there was a huge meeting in Washington, DC. It was called the *March on Washington*. Thousands of people came. African Americans and white people who wanted civil rights for everyone were there. Dr. Martin Luther King Jr. gave his famous "I Have a Dream" speech. He said that he dreamed of a time when all people were equal and happy. Parks was there, too.

The next year, President Lyndon B. Johnson signed the Civil Rights Act. It was a new law that said all people had to be treated equally. Parks was happy that there would finally be fair laws.

March on Washington, 1963

Dr. Martin Luther King Jr.

President Johnson signs the Civil Rights Act in 1964.

The Mother of Civil Rights

In 1996, President Bill Clinton gave Parks the Presidential (prez-i-DEN-shuhl) Medal of Freedom. In 1999, Congress gave her the Congressional (kuhn-GRESH-uh-nl) Gold Medal. These are the highest honors for an American **citizen**.

President Clinton gives Parks the Presidential Medal of Freedom.

People gather around Parks's casket to pay their respects.

Parks was honored with this U.S. postage stamp.

2013

Rosa Parks

In 2005, Parks passed away. She was 92 years old. Her body was brought to the U.S. **Capitol** building. This is where Congress meets. She was the first woman to be honored in this way. More than 4,000 people came to pay their respects to her.

People remember Parks for refusing to give up her seat on a bus. But she did so much more. She worked her entire life to help make things fair for all people. She is known as the Mother of Civil Rights.

Amazing Americans Today

Rosa Parks was an amazing American. She stood up for what she believed in and never gave up. Today, there are many amazing Americans. They help people, too.

Judy is Scott's amazing American. She is a veterinarian. She works with animals from shelters. As a veterinarian, she cares for animals who cannot speak for themselves.

Write It!

Think of an amazing American that you know. What does he or she do to help your community? Draw a picture and write a paragraph about why you think this person is an amazing American.

Scott drew this picture of Judy caring for a dog.

Glossary

bail—an amount of money given to a court to allow someone to leave jail and return for a trial

boycott—when people refuse to buy, use, or participate in something as a way of protesting

Capitol—the building in which the people who make the laws for the United States meet

citizen—a person who legally belongs to a country

civil rights—rights that every person should have

Congress—the group of people who are responsible for making the laws of a country

court—a place where cases are heard

elected—chosen by voting

equal—the same

lawyer—a person whose job is to guide and assist people in matters relating to the law

segregation—the practice of separating groups of people because of their race or religion

slaves—people who are owned by another and have no freedom

Index

Your Turn!

Inspiration

Rosa Parks was an inspiration to many people. She inspired others to stand up for change. What do you think is unfair today? Talk to your friends and family about something that is unfair. Then, write about what you can do to help change it.